"Don Whitney's suggestion to pray the Bible has made a huge contribution to my devotional life. This little book is explosive and powerful. Read it ready to experience a great step forward in your walk with Christ and in your commitment to prayer."

R. Albert Mohler Jr., President and Joseph Emerson Brown
Professor of Christian Theology, The Southern Baptist Theological
Seminary

"My walk with the Lord has often been strengthened and encouraged by Don Whitney's writing. Now he reminds us of the value of using Scripture as a prompt and basis for our prayers. This is a particularly helpful tool for those of us who often struggle to know what and how to pray or whose minds tend to wander during private prayer. This book will surely help many refresh their time with the Lord."

Nancy DeMoss Wolgemuth, author; radio host, *Revive Our Hearts*

"If you are looking for a book to teach you not only to pray but also to invigorate your intimacy with God through prayer, this is the one. I highly recommend this book written by a man who has instructed thousands of people about spiritual disciplines in academic circles and in church settings. My soul has been nourished as I have sat under Whitney's teaching, especially on the topic of prayer. You and I need this book. You will be blessed in more than one way."

Miguel Núñez, Senior Pastor, International Baptist Church of
Santo Domingo; President, Wisdom and Integrity

"I prayed through Psalm 23 with tears streaming down my face, asking myself, why have I not done this before? Perhaps you've been told to pray the Scriptures, but you haven't because you were never taught *how* to. Whitney's simple approach makes praying through the Bible accessible while also leaving space for the Word and Spirit to work in your heart. Don't give up on prayer! *Praying the Bible* will help transform your prayer life."

Trillia Newbell, author, *United: Captured by God's Vision for
Diversity* and *Fear and Faith*

"Prayer and Scripture intake are both essential for spiritual devotion, like the left and right wings of a plane. Prayer is the Christian's duty. It should also be the Christian's delight. *Praying the Bible* will teach you to take in the joy of Scripture-led prayer."

H. B. Charles Jr., Pastor, Shiloh Metropolitan Baptist Church, Jacksonville, Florida

"Whitney offers a wonderfully practical, pastoral, and biblical approach to prayer that relieves personal boredom and unleashes spiritual power. It's so simple it will shock you and, at the same time, invigorate a renewed prayer life with your God."

Bryan Chapell, President Emeritus, Covenant Theological Seminary; Senior Pastor, Grace Presbyterian Church, Peoria, Illinois

"Whitney has taught the material in this book a number of times at the WorshipGod conferences I lead. Unfailingly his has been one of the most appreciated and life-affecting seminars we've offered. I can't recommend this book highly enough."

Bob Kauflin, Director of Worship, Sovereign Grace Ministries; author, *Worship Matters* and *True Worshipers*

Praying the Bible

PRAYING

THE

BIBLE

DONALD S. WHITNEY

:: **CROSSWAY**®

WHEATON, ILLINOIS

Library of Congress Cataloging-in-Publication Data

Whitney, Donald S., (Professor)
Praying the Bible / Donald S. Whitney.
    pages cm
    Includes bibliographical references and index.
    ISBN 978-1-4335-4784-3 (hc)
    1. Prayer—Christianity. 2. Bible—Devotional use. I. Title.
BV215.W465   2015
248.3'2—dc23   2014046060

Crossway is a publishing ministry of Good News Publishers.

LB		29	28	27	26	25	24	23	22	21	20
22	21	20	19	18	17	16	15	14	13	12	11

For T. W. Hunt, the most prayerful man I've ever known. Thank you for decades of daily prayer for me.

And also for R. F. Gates, whom God used in ways neither of us could have ever imagined in that moment on March 1, 1985, when you held up the Bible and said, "When you pray, use the prayer book!"

And most of all, for my Lord and Savior, Jesus Christ.

All this, indeed all of life, is for you and about you. After talking with you so many thousands of times, I can't wait to see you.

Contents

1

The Problem

If I try to pray for people or events without having the word in front of me guiding my prayers, then several negative things happen. One is that I tend to be very repetitive. . . . I just pray the same things all the time. Another negative thing is that my mind tends to wander.

John Piper

Since prayer is talking with God, why don't people pray more? Why don't the people of God *enjoy* prayer more? I maintain that people—truly born-again, genuinely Christian people—often do not pray simply because they do not *feel* like it. And the reason they don't feel like praying is that when they do pray, they tend to say the same old things about the same old things.

When you've said the same old things about the same old things about a thousand times, how do you feel about saying them again? Did you dare just think the "B" word? Yes, bored. We can be talking to the most fascinating Person in the universe about the most important things in our lives and be bored to death.

As a result, a great many Christians conclude, "It must be me. Something's wrong with me. If I get bored in something as important as prayer, then I must be a second-rate Christian."

Indeed, why would people become bored when talking with God, especially when talking about that which is most important to them? Is it because we don't love God? Is it because, deep down, we really care nothing for the people or matters we pray about? No. Rather, if this mind-wandering boredom describes your experience in prayer, I would argue that if you are indwelled by the Holy Spirit—if you are born again—then the problem is not you; it is your *method*.

The Spirit's Presence Prompts Prayer

Notice that very important condition—"if you are indwelled by the Holy Spirit"—for no method will enliven prayer for a person who isn't indwelled by the Holy Spirit. Such a person has no sustained appetite for prayer, no long-term desire for it.

When God brings someone into a relationship with himself through Jesus Christ, he begins to live within that person by means of his Holy Spirit. As the apostle Paul writes to followers of Jesus in Ephesians 1:13, "In him you also, when you heard the word of truth, the gospel of your salvation, and believed in him, were sealed with the promised Holy Spirit." In 1 Corinthians 6:19 Paul also reassures believers in Christ, "Your body is a temple of the Holy Spirit within you, whom you have from God."

Just as you bring your human nature with you whenever you enter any place, so whenever the Holy Spirit enters any person, he brings his holy nature with him. The result is that all those in whom the Spirit dwells have new holy hungers and holy loves they did not have prior to having his indwelling presence. They hunger for the holy Word of God, which they used to find boring or irrelevant (1 Pet. 2:2). They love fellowship with the people of God, finding it unimaginable to live apart from meaningful interaction with them (1 John 3:14). Hearts and minds in which the Holy Spirit dwells feel holy longings unknown to them previously. They long to live in a holy body without sin, yearn for a holy mind no longer subject to temptation, groan for a holy world filled with holy people, and earnestly desire to see at last the face of the one the angels call "Holy, holy, holy" (Rev. 4:8).

This is the spiritual heartbeat of 100 percent of the hearts where the Spirit of God lives. A person may be just nine years old, but if the Holy Spirit has come to him or her, then these hungers and desires are planted there (expressed in nine-year-old ways, of course, but they live there because he lives there). And a person may be ninety-nine with a heart encrusted by the traditions and experiences of the years, but pulsing underneath is the ever-fresh, ever-green work of the Holy Spirit manifested in every person in whom he dwells.

And according to the New Testament letters of both Romans and Galatians, another of the supernatural heart changes the Spirit creates in all Christians is to cause them to cry, "Abba! Father!" (Rom. 8:15; Gal. 4:6).[1] Thus when someone is born again, the Holy Spirit gives that person new Fatherward desires, a new heavenward orientation whereby we cry, "Abba, Father!" In other words, all those indwelled by the Holy Spirit really want to pray. The Holy Spirit causes all the children of God to believe that God is their Father and fills them with an undying desire to talk to him.

"Something Must Be Wrong with Me"

Nevertheless, while this Spirit-produced passion is pushing against one side of our soul, colliding with that is our experience. And our experience says, "But when I pray, frankly, it's boring." And when prayer is boring, we don't feel like praying. And when we don't feel like praying, it's hard to make ourselves pray. Even five or six minutes of prayer can feel like an eternity. Our mind wanders half the time. We'll suddenly come to ourselves and think, "Now where was I? I haven't been thinking of God for the last several minutes." And we'll return to that mental script we've repeated countless times. But almost immediately our minds begin to wander again because we've said the same old things about the same old things so many times.

"It must be me," we conclude. "Prayer isn't supposed to be like this. I guess I'm just a second-rate Christian."

No, the problem is almost certainly not you; it's your method. If you have turned from living for yourself and your sin and have trusted Jesus Christ and his work to make you right with God, God has given you the Holy Spirit. And if you are seeking to live under the lordship of Jesus Christ and the authority of God's Word (the Bible), confessing known sin and fighting the lifelong tendency to sin instead of excusing it, then the problem of boredom in prayer is not you; rather, it is your method.

And the method of most Christians in prayer is to say the same old things about the same old things. After forty years of experience in ministry, I am convinced that this problem is almost universal. Virtually from the beginning of their Christian life, it seems that nearly every believer suffers from this habit.

When prayer consists of the same spoken sentences on every occasion, naturally we wonder at the value of the practice. If our prayers bore us, do they also bore God? Does God really need to hear me say these things again? We can begin to feel like a little girl I heard about. Her parents had taught her the classic bedtime prayer for children that begins, "Now I lay me down to sleep." One night she thought, "Why does God need to hear me say this again?" So she decided to record herself saying the prayer, and then she played the recording each night when she went to bed.

Perhaps you smile at her story, but you have prayer recordings in your head; they're just a little longer or more sophisticated. Recorded in your memory are prayers—your own or the prayers of others—you can repeat mindlessly.

I pastored a church in the Chicago area for almost fifteen years. During the worship service one Sunday morning the ushers came forward to receive the offering, and one of the ushers was asked to pray. As the man was praying, I could hear someone else talking. I thought, *Surely this person will stop in a moment.* Then I realized it was a child, and I said to myself, *Some adult will quiet this child any second now.* But as the talking continued, I opened my eyes and saw in the second row the five-year-old son of the usher who was praying. Soon it became obvious that the little boy was praying the same words as his dad; not repeating after him but in unison with him. It was like when entire congregations pray the Lord's Prayer in unison; instead this was a father and son praying "Dad's prayer." How could such a little boy do that? It was because every time his dad prayed, whether at the Lord's Supper table at the church or the supper table at home, his dad prayed the same prayer. The boy had been in the world only sixty months, and he had already memorized everything his dad said when he prayed. He could say the words of the prayer, but most of what came out of his mouth was just a repetition of what were, to his five-year-old mind, empty phrases.

There may be people in your own family, or your church, or somewhere in your background who, when they were or are called upon to pray, *you* could give the prayer because you've heard it so many times. Our hearts don't soar when we hear such praying; we just politely endure it.

One prayer does not a prayer life make. Prayers without variety eventually become words without meaning. Jesus said that to pray this way is to pray in vain, for in the Sermon on the Mount he warned, "When you pray, do not heap up empty phrases as the Gentiles do, for they think that they will be heard for their many words" (Matt. 6:7).

The tragedy is that too often that's the way it is with our own prayers. We believe in prayer, and the Spirit of God prompts us to pray, but because we always say the same old things about the same old things, it can seem as though all we do in prayer is simply "heap up empty phrases." Although this drains most of the motivation from talking with God, we'll dutifully try to grind out another round of prayer; yet our minds constantly wander from the words, and we condemn ourselves as spiritual failures.

Praying about "the Same Old Things" Is Normal

Notice carefully—for this is very important—that the problem is *not* that we pray *about* the same old things. To routinely pray about the same people and situations is perfectly normal. It's normal to pray about the same old things because our lives tend to consist of the same old things.

For example, if I came to your church or Bible study group and randomly selected a handful of people, including you, then asked each person to get alone and spend the next five to ten minutes in prayer, I'm confident that nearly every person in the group would pray about the same half dozen things.

Each person would likely pray about his or her *family* in one sense or another. Married people would pray for their spouses, singles might pray to be married, parents would pray for their children, and so forth.

Doubtless everyone would pray about their *future*, perhaps asking for direction about some decision, such as a change at work or whether to move to a new place. Or their prayer might be about an upcoming event or some life change that's on their horizon.

It's very likely all would pray about their *finances*, seeking God's provision for that car, for those bills, or for school.

Most would pray about their *work*, or if students, they'd pray in some way about their schoolwork. It's normal for people to pray in regard to what they spend most of their waking hours doing during the week.

Each of these believers would probably pray about some *Christian concern*, such as something related to their church or to a personal ministry involvement with someone. Possibly they would pray for a brother or sister in Christ who is suffering or for someone with whom they are trying to share the gospel.

And then each one would almost certainly pray about the *current crisis* in his or her life. I have read that each of us experiences a relatively significant crisis on an average of once every six months or so. The matter may be a good thing or a bad thing, a birth or a death, a job change you want or one you don't want, but it's such a big deal that when you pray, it's one of the first things that comes to mind. This situation devours so much of your attention that you need no prayer list to remind you to pray about it.

If you are going to pray about your life, these six things *are* your life, aren't they? If you don't think so, how much of your life is not at all related to your family, your future, your finances, your work or schoolwork, your Christian concerns, and the current crisis? These are the areas where you devote almost all your time. Moreover, these are the great loves of your life, the places where your heart is.

And, thankfully, these things don't change dramatically very often. Families, for example, don't experience the changes of marriages, births, and deaths month after month, year in and year out. While there may be frequent small changes in these areas, really big changes in our family, work, etc., usually don't happen every week or even every month.

So, if you are going to pray about your life, and if these

six things *are* your life, and if these things don't change significantly very often, that means you are going to pray *about* the same old things most of the time. That's normal.

Saying "the Same Old Things" Is Boring

Therefore the problem is not that we pray *about* the same old things; rather, it's that we *say* the same old things about the same old things. It seems that virtually everyone begins to pray this way sooner or later, and it is boring. And when prayer is boring, we don't feel like praying. When we don't feel like praying, it's hard to pray, at least in any sort of focused, heartfelt way.

That's when we are tempted to think, *It must be me. I must be just a second-rate Christian.*

The natural response to such discouragement can be, "Then stop it! Quit praying. Why do this to yourself? If prayer is so boring and leaves you so frustrated and disheartened, then don't pray anymore."

A true Christian would recoil, astonished at such a suggestion. No matter how boring a believer's prayer life, no matter how few prayers are answered, no matter how deep the sense of failure in prayer, anyone indwelled by the Holy Spirit can never permanently give up prayer. That's the result of the ongoing ministry of the third person of the Trinity, which is referred to by theologians as the "preserving work" of the Holy Spirit. Once the Spirit of God brings people to spiritual life, he preserves them in that life, granting them the grace to persevere in the evidences of that life, such as prayer. In other words, once the Spirit causes a person to begin to cry, "Abba! Father!" he continues creating Godward looks and pleas in that person forever.

So, due to the ongoing work of the Holy Spirit, you believe in prayer and you really want to pray. But when you try to pray, it just feels like, well, like something's wrong. Then perhaps you hear a sermon on prayer, or you hear a testimony about answered prayer, or you read a book (like this one) on prayer, and for a while you go back to prayer, recommitted and rejuvenated but basically still saying the same old things about the same old things, just with a bit more spiritual "oomph" behind it. Very soon, though, the new enthusiasm evaporates, and you find that saying the same old things about the same old things is as boring as before, only now you feel guiltier than ever because you had been so resolved that things would be different this time.

Once again you return to what seems the inevitable conclusion: "It must be me. Something's wrong with me. I must be just a second-rate Christian."

2

The Solution

Nothing has brought more vigor, satisfaction, and consistency to my own prayers as this single discipline.

Is there a solution? If so, it has to be fundamentally simple. Since God invites—indeed, if by his Spirit he enables—all his children to pray, then prayer must be essentially simple. God has children all over the world, as diverse as people can be—from age nine to ninety-nine, some with low IQs and some with high IQs, some with no formal education and some with the highest levels of formal education. And most of them are ordinary folks, not primarily those whom the world considers intellectual or cultural elite. As the apostle Paul put it, "Consider your calling, brothers: not many of you were wise according to worldly standards" (1 Cor. 1:26).

Every Christian Can Have a Meaningful, Satisfying Prayer Life

Although God doesn't choose many who are "wise according to worldly standards," he does call people from every imaginable circumstance and background. Our Father draws to himself people with few Christian resources and people with many Christian resources, such as those who aren't able even to own a Bible and those who own many; those who do not live near a good, healthy church and those who experience rich fellowship and sound biblical exposition every week; those who cannot read or who have no Christian books and those for whom many Christian books are readily available; those who have no access to Christian teaching by means of various media and those who do. But if God invites and expects all his children—regardless of their age, IQ, education, or resources—to do the same thing—to pray—then prayer has to be simple.

Therefore, it must be possible for every Christian, including every Christian reading this book, to have a meaningful, satisfying prayer life. For if you with all your Christian resources—presumably a Bible, a church family, the availability of Christian books, access to Christian teaching via radio and the Internet, and more—if *you* can't have a fulfilling prayer life in spite of all these helps, then what hope is there for our brothers and sisters in isolated locations, lands where non-Christian religions dominate, or places of persecution where few, if any, of these Christian resources are available?

Are you ready to say, "Well, that's pretty tight logic, for if I, despite my education, experience, and all my Christian resources, don't seem capable of a meaningful, satisfying prayer life, then that necessarily implies that almost no Christian in the world can enjoy one either, since almost no follower of Jesus anywhere has as many of these helps for prayer as I"?

No. Of course not. You'd never say that. Instead, you're more likely to think, *Look, I don't know about anybody else. I just know that when I pray, it's boring. So it must be me. There's something wrong with me. In fact, now that you've shown me all the advantages I have in comparison to many other Christians in the world, I feel guiltier than ever. I felt like a failure in prayer before, but apparently I'm even worse than I thought. Thanks a lot! Boy, I'm sure glad that I picked up this book!*

So now we've come to the most challenging part of this book. It's possible that you have been saying the same old things about the same old things in prayer for so long that it's hard for you to believe that you could easily learn to pray any other way, as though you were listening to a lung specialist say that you could easily change the way you breathe. Many who are reading this book have endured the guilt of an incurably wandering mind and feelings of boredom in prayer for decades, and here comes a writer asking you to believe that there is a simple, permanent, biblical solution to a problem that's plagued you for most of your life. Would I really ask you to believe that?

Yes, that's exactly what I'm saying.

I do realize that after all these years of unsatisfying prayer, you might find it challenging to believe that the problem is not you, Christian, but your method. But once again, let's return to the facts. The Lord has his people all over the world, and among them are believers of every sort of demographic description. And yet by his Spirit, he gives to all of them a desire to pray. Would he do this for all if meaningful prayer was doable only by some? Would your heavenly Father make prayer so difficult or confusing that you could never enjoy it or, rather, never enjoy him through prayer? Despite his love for his people, a love demonstrated by the incarnation and crucifixion of his Son for them, a love made evident by providing the Holy Spirit and the Bible and the church, would he then devise a means of communion between himself and his children that most would find to be a frustrating, boring monotony?

That makes no sense. What does make sense is that the Father, who wanted to enjoy fellowship with all his children and wanted all his children to enjoy talking with him, would make it simple for all to do so.

The Simple, Permanent, Biblical Solution

So what is the simple solution to the boring routine of saying the same old things about the same old things? Here it is: *when you pray, pray through a passage of Scripture, particularly a psalm.*

That probably didn't seem as dramatic as you were expecting. In fact, you may have heard something similar to this before. If so, it was most likely when someone teaching through one of the prayers of the apostle Paul (e.g., Eph. 1:15–23; 3:14–21; Phil. 1:9–11) said, "We should pray these prayers today." And I agree; we should. Better yet, though, I believe we should pray everything in Paul's letters, not just his prayers.

The best place, however, for learning to pray through a passage of Scripture is in the book of Psalms.

3

The Method

The Psalms: they are designed to be prayed.

Gordon Wenham

Now we're going to see what praying through a psalm looks like. Let's use the twenty-third psalm as an example. And let's say that, as is probably true in real life, you read your Bible first. Perhaps you read in Matthew, or in Hebrews, and then you turn to prayer. You decide to pray through a psalm, and you choose Psalm 23. You read the first verse—"The LORD is my shepherd"—and you pray something like this:

Lord, I thank you that you *are* my shepherd. You're a good shepherd. You have shepherded me all my life. And, great Shepherd, please shepherd my family today: guard them from the ways of the world; guide them into the ways of God. Lead them not into temptation; deliver them from evil. O great Shepherd, I pray for my children; cause them to be your sheep. May they love you as their shepherd, as I do. And, Lord, please shepherd me in the decision that's before me about my future. Do I make that move, that change, or not? I also pray for our under-shepherds at the church. Please shepherd them as they shepherd us.

And you continue praying anything else that comes to mind as you consider the words, "The LORD is my shepherd." Then when nothing else comes to mind, you go to the next line: "I shall not want." And perhaps you pray:

Lord, I thank you that I've never really been in want. I haven't missed too many meals. All that I am and all that I have has come from you. But I know it pleases you that I bring my desires to you, so would you provide the finances that we need for those bills, for school, for that car?

Maybe you know someone who is in want, and you pray for God's provision for him or her. Or you remember some of our persecuted brothers and sisters around the world, and you pray for their concerns.

After you've finished, you look at the next verse: "He makes me lie down in green pastures" (v. 2a). And, frankly, when you read the words "lie down," maybe what comes to mind is simply, "Lord, I would be grateful if you would make it possible for me to lie down and take a nap today."[2]

Possibly the term "green pastures" makes you think of the feeding of God's flock in the green pastures of his Word, and it prompts you to pray for a Bible teaching ministry you lead, or for a teacher or pastor who feeds you with the Word of God. When was the last time you did that? Maybe you have never done that, but praying through this psalm caused you to do so.

Next you read, "He leads me beside still waters" (v. 2b). And maybe you begin to plead,

> Yes, Lord, do lead me in that decision I have to make about my future. I want to do what *you* want, O Lord, but I don't know what that is. Please lead me into your will in this matter. And lead me beside *still* waters in this. Please quiet the anxious waters in my soul about this situation. Let me experience your peace. May the turbulence in my heart be stilled by trust in you and your sovereignty over all things and over all people.

Following that, you read these words from verse 3, "He restores my soul." That prompts you to pray along the lines of:

> My Shepherd, I come to you so spiritually dry today. Please restore my soul; restore to me the joy of your salvation. And I pray you will restore the soul of that person from work/school/down the street with whom I'm hoping to share the gospel. Please restore his soul from darkness to light, from death to life.

You can continue praying in this way until either (1) you run out of time, or (2) you run out of psalm. And if you run out of psalm before you run out of time, you simply turn the page and go to another psalm. By so doing, you never run out of anything to say, and, best of all, *you never again say the same old things about the same old things.*

So basically what you are doing is taking words that originated in the heart and mind of God and circulating them through your heart and mind back to God. By this means his words become the wings of your prayers.

4

More about the Method

Open the Bible, start reading it, and pause at every verse and turn it into a prayer.

John Piper

To pray the Bible, you simply go through the passage line by line, talking to God about whatever comes to mind as you read the text. See how easy that is? Anyone can do that.

If you don't understand the meaning of a verse, go on to the next verse. If the meaning of that one is perfectly clear but nothing comes to mind to pray about, go on to the next verse. Just speak to the Lord about everything that occurs to you as you slowly read his Word. You do this even if—and this page of the book is potentially the one most likely to be misunderstood—even if what comes to mind has nothing to do with the text.

Now, let me defend that biblically. What does the text of Scripture tell us to pray about? Everything, right? The

Bible tells us that in Philippians 4:6: "Do not be anxious about anything, but in everything by prayer and supplication with thanksgiving let your requests be made known to God." We may bring "everything by prayer" to God. Everything is something we may pray about. Every person, every object, every issue, every circumstance, every fear, every situation—everything in the universe is something we may bring before God. So every thought that enters your mind as you are reading a passage of Scripture—even if that thought has nothing to do with the text before you at the moment—is something you may bring to God.

Interpreting the Bible versus Praying the Bible

I want to make a crucial distinction between what I wrote in the previous paragraph and interpreting the Bible accurately, a process formally known as "hermeneutics." Correctly handling the Word of God does not permit making the text say what we want. To understand the Bible accurately—which is essential for right belief and living, for truthful sharing with others, and for authoritative teaching and preaching—we must do whatever is necessary to discover (or "exegete") the single, God-inspired meaning of every verse before us. The text of the Bible means what God inspired it to mean, not "what it means to me."

When we come to the Bible on all other occasions I can think of, our primary purpose is to understand and apply it. So let's say we are doing Bible study. *Primarily* we are putting in the mental effort (and perhaps physical effort too, if we are using other reference tools) to understand what the text before us says and means. *Secondarily* we are praying. "Lord," we might ask from time to time, "what does this mean?" or occasionally pray, "How do I apply this?"

As I said, that's our mind-set, more or less, on almost all occasions when we come to the Bible, whether it's a deeper level of Bible study or simply the daily reading of one or more chapters of Scripture.

But that's not what we're doing here.

With what I'm advocating, our *primary* activity is prayer, not Bible intake. Bible reading is *secondary* in this process. Our focus is on God through prayer; our glance is at the Bible. And we turn Godward and pray about every matter that occurs to us as we read. Do you see the distinction?

Let me use a ridiculous illustration to make the point. Suppose you are praying through Psalm 130, and you come to verse 3: "If you, O LORD, should mark iniquities, O Lord, who could stand?" And when you see that verb "mark," your friend Mark comes to mind. What should you do? Pray for Mark! You know that verse is not about Mark, but it's certainly not wrong to pray for Mark just because he popped into your head as you were reading Psalm 130:3.

Here's a more realistic illustration. Let's return to a verse from which we prayed a few moments ago, Psalm 23:3:

"He restores my soul." I said that one of the things this verse might prompt you to pray for is the salvation of a person with whom you are trying to share the gospel, to pray that God would restore that person's soul from darkness to light, from death to life. If I were to *preach* on Psalm 23 and say, "This verse is about evangelism; about God restoring the souls of those in spiritual darkness," I would be sinning. That verse is not about evangelism, and I know it. It's about a believer's soul being restored to the joy of God's salvation. Were I to declare to others that God's Word here means one thing when I know it means another would be, at best, to misuse the text. We never have the right to claim that the Bible says something it does not.

But if, while you are *praying* through Psalm 23:3, your non-Christian friend comes to mind, and you use the language of this verse to say, "Lord, restore my friend's soul; restore him from darkness to light, from death to life," that's fine. This isn't *reading something into* the text; it's merely *using the language of* the text to speak to God about what has come into your mind.

So, again, simply turn every thought Godward as you read the passage. At some points you will pray exactly what the text is about, as when you pray, "Lord, restore my soul to the joy of your salvation." At other times you will use biblical language to pray thoughts unrelated to the text that come to you while reading the text, as in, "Lord, restore my non-Christian friend's soul from death to life."

Confidence in the Word and the Spirit

I have enough confidence in the Word and the Spirit of God to believe that if people will pray in this way, in the long run their prayers will be far more biblical than if they just make up their own prayers. That's what people usually do: make up their own prayers. What's the result? We tend to say the same old things about the same old things. And without the Scripture to shape our prayers, we are far more likely to pray in unbiblical ways than if we pray the thoughts that occur to us as we read the Scripture. So while it's true that people may use this method and pray about things that are not found in the text, I contend that will happen much less if people will pray while reading the text. By this means, the Spirit of God will use the Word of God to help the people of God pray increasingly according to the will of God.

I think it's important enough to say it again: regardless of how far from the true meaning of the text people's minds and therefore their prayers may wander, I have enough confidence in the Word and the Spirit of God to believe that if people will pray in this way, in the long run their prayers will be far more biblical than if they just make up their own prayers. Moreover, is there any better way for people to learn the true meaning of the text—if they are alone with the Holy Spirit and the Bible—than to pray over the text? The godly nineteenth-century Scottish pastor Robert Murray M'Cheyne affirmed this when he said, "*Turn the*

Bible into prayer. . . . This is the best way of knowing the meaning of the Bible, and of learning to pray."[3]

In reality, I think that most of the time people will pray fairly close to the true meaning of the text, for if they don't understand a verse while praying through a passage, they'll probably move on to the next verse that they do understand. I've given these illustrations not to excuse someone's laziness in handling the text but rather to show that even in the case where a person prays about a matter far removed from the proper interpretation of the text, it's acceptable to speak to God about such matters. People should feel free to pray about whatever comes to mind as they read through a passage of Scripture.

A Simple Method

That's it. If you are praying through a psalm, you simply read that psalm line by line, talking to God about whatever thoughts are prompted by the inspired words you read. If your mind wanders from the subject of the text, take those wandering thoughts Godward, then return to the text. If you come to a verse you don't understand, just skip it and go to the next verse. If you don't understand that one, move on. If you do understand it but nothing comes to mind to pray about, go to the next verse. If sinful thoughts enter in, pray about them and go on. You may read twenty or thirty verses in that psalm, and yet on a given day have only five or six things come to mind. No problem. Nothing says you have to pray over every verse. Nothing says you have to finish the psalm.

I was teaching this method at a church in Santa Rosa, California, and gave the people an opportunity to try praying through a passage of Scripture. One woman prayed for twenty-five minutes and never got past "The LORD is my shepherd." For nearly half an hour she talked to the Lord about those five words. Do you think that in heaven the Lord was saying, in a huff, "You didn't finish the psalm!"? No, I think he was delighted that she found so much delight in him as her shepherd that she could talk to him for twenty-five minutes about that, regardless of whether she prayed through the rest of the psalm. At other times, though—and this is probably more common—you will go through many verses and only a few matters will come to mind. Fine; just keep turning the page.

Imprecatory Psalms

You'll come to those sections known as the "imprecatory psalms," those passages where the psalmist calls for God's judgment upon his enemies—people also presumed to be God's enemies. But how do you pray through a psalm when it contains verses like these:

> Blessed shall he be who takes your little ones
> and dashes them against the rock! (Ps. 137:9)

> O God, break the teeth in their mouths! (Ps. 58:6)

Let them be like the snail that dissolves into slime.
(Ps. 58:8)

Well, maybe there's someone at work for whom you are
tempted momentarily to pray such things, but it's difficult
to do with a pure motive, isn't it? While I believe those
sections of Scripture are inspired as fully as John 3:16 and
any other part of the Bible, I don't think we should pray
verses like these with specific people in mind. To do that
would be hard to reconcile with Jesus's command in Matthew 5:44–45, "Love your enemies and pray for those who
persecute you, so that you may be sons of your Father who
is in heaven."

I do think we can put specific sins in those passages,
praying that God will smash their teeth as they attempt
to devour our souls. I sometimes pray angrily that all the
enemies of God born in my sinful heart will be destroyed
as thoroughly as these imprecatory psalms describe. I also
believe we can pray these imprecations against national
sins, as I sometimes do, for example, against abortion and
racism. Ultimately, as we view the Scriptures Christocentri-
cally, we can put such psalms in the mouth of Jesus. Someday he is going to do far worse than just break the teeth in
the mouth of his lifelong, unrepentant enemies. Essentially
we can pray these psalms in such a way that reflects the
attitude, "Lord, I am on your side and against all your
enemies. I want your justice and righteousness to win the
final victory over sin and rebellion against you."

But let's say that one day next week as you are praying through a psalm, you come to one of these sections. You might think, "That Whitney guy in the book on *Praying the Bible* said we could pray through these kinds of psalms, but I don't remember what he said." That's okay. Maybe you'll pray, "Lord, what does this mean?" or "Please show me how I can pray from this passage." Perhaps you'll move past the entire section and go to the next verse that gives you clear direction in prayer. Any of this is fine. That's why this method is so simple, and anyone can do it.

Some of the Benefits

It's not only easy to *begin* praying with this method; this method makes it easy to *continue* in prayer. The basic spirituality course I teach in seminary is called "Personal Spiritual Disciplines." On the first day of class I announce that once during the semester, each student is to spend four consecutive hours alone with God. When I say this, the concern I read on many faces tells me that they are thinking, *What am I going to do for four hours?* But after I teach them how to meditate on Scripture and how to pray through a passage of Scripture, most of them spend the entire four hours alternating between those two activities, sometimes writing their meditations or prayers in a journal. What's so encouraging is that nearly all the students spend more than four hours on the assignment—not because they have to but because they are enjoying it so much that they don't want to stop. Many of them walk while praying through a psalm, and if they reach the end of the psalm but want to keep walking and praying, they simply turn the page and continue praying.

Praying the Bible in this way is so practical because it expands or contracts to accommodate however much or how little time you have for prayer. So it works if you have four hours, like those students, and yet it works if you have just four minutes. If you have only four minutes, you won't get very far in the text, but you can still pray the Bible. Conversely, if you have four hours for prayer, you just keep turning the page. No matter how long you pray, you never run out of things to pray when you pray the Bible.

Even better is the fact that when you pray through a passage of Scripture, you don't pray empty, repetitive phrases. Talk to God about the words you read in the Bible, and you'll never again pray the same old things about the same old things. That alone is worth the time you've invested in reading this book, isn't it?

But it gets even better than that, because the words you use when you pray the Bible are not just fresh, new phrases you haven't used in prayer before, as energizing as that is. Praying from the Word of God means your prayers include *inspired* words. As Joni Eareckson Tada explains:

I have learned to . . . season my prayers with the word of God. It's a way of talking to God in his language—speaking his dialect, using his vernacular, employing his idioms. . . . This is not a matter simply of divine vocabulary. It's a matter of power. When we bring God's word directly into our praying, we are bringing God's power into our praying. Hebrews 4:12 declares, "For the word of God is living and active. Sharper than any double-edged sword." God's word is living, and so it infuses our prayers with life and vitality. God's word is also active, injecting energy and power into our prayer.[4]

There is a supernatural quality to the words of Scripture that you pray. Jesus said, "The words that I have spoken to you are spirit and life" (John 6:63). When you pray the Bible, you aren't just praying ordinary words; you are praying words of spirit and life.

5

Praying the Psalms

By praying the Psalms back to God, we learn to pray in tune with the Father, Son, and Holy Spirit.

As a whole, the psalms comprise the best place in Scripture from which to pray Scripture. I base that on the original purpose for which God inspired the psalms. The book of Psalms—which means "book of praises" in Hebrew—was the songbook of Israel. The psalms were inspired by God for the purpose of being sung to God.

It is as though God said to his people, "I want you to praise me, but you don't know how to praise me. I want you to praise me not because I'm an egomaniac but because you will praise that which you prize the most, and there is nothing of greater worth to you than I. There is nothing more praiseworthy than I, and it is a blessing for you to know that. It will lead to your eternal joy if you praise me above all others and above all else and to your eternal misery if you do not. But there's a problem. You don't know how to praise me, at least not in a way that's fully true and pleasing to me. In fact, you know nothing about me unless I reveal it to you, for I am invisible to you. Therefore, since I want you to praise me, and it is good for you to praise me, but since you don't know how to praise me, here are the words I want you to use."

Why the Psalms?

In other words, God gave the Psalms to us so that we would give the Psalms back to God. No other book of the Bible was inspired for that expressed purpose.

In addition, we know that singing the Psalms continues to be pleasing to God and edifying to his people today, for in two key New Testament passages (Eph. 5:18–19 and Col. 3:16) a healthy church is characterized by singing "psalms and hymns and spiritual songs."[5] So in the Psalms God teaches us to come before him using words such as:

You, O LORD, are a shield about me. (Ps. 3:3)

O LORD, our Lord,
   how majestic is your name in all the earth!
You have set your glory above the heavens. (Ps. 8:1)

You make known to me the path of life;
   in your presence there is fullness of joy;

at your right hand are pleasures forevermore.
    (Ps. 16:11)

How precious is your steadfast love, O God! (Ps. 36:7)

A broken and contrite heart, O God, you will not despise. (Ps. 51:17)

Your righteousness, O God,
    reaches the high heavens.
You who have done great things,
    O God, who is like you? (Ps. 71:19)

Your way, O God, is holy.
    What god is great like our God? (Ps. 77:13)

You, O Lord, are good and forgiving,
    abounding in steadfast love to all who call
        upon you. (Ps. 86:5)

O LORD my God, you are very great!
You are clothed with splendor and majesty,
    covering yourself with light as with a garment,
    stretching out the heavens like a tent.
        (Ps. 104:1–2)

Your word is a lamp to my feet
    and a light to my path. (Ps. 119:105)

O LORD, you have searched me and known me!
You know when I sit down and when I rise up;
    you discern my thoughts from afar. (Ps. 139:1–2)

Your kingdom is an everlasting kingdom,
and your dominion endures throughout all
generations. (Ps. 145:13)

Have you considered the Psalms from this perspective? That is, for our good and his glory, God wants us to praise him. And, indeed, all those indwelled by his Spirit yearn to praise him. But we have no way of knowing what sort of praises are worthy of our glorious God. So he revealed in the Psalms the praises that express the yearnings his Spirit produces in us and which are appropriate for and consistent with his glory. As we pray the Psalms, therefore, we are returning to God words that he expressly inspired for us to speak and sing to him.

The "Psalms of the Day"

I want to commend to you a systematic approach for praying a psalm each day. The approach did not originate with me, but I can't recall where I first encountered the concept decades ago. It's called "Psalms of the Day." Before I explain how it works, here's why I think it's worth your time to learn it. If you intend to pray through a psalm, using the Psalms of the Day approach helps you avoid thumbing through the middle of your Bible, randomly searching for a psalm that looks interesting. Too often, such an inconsistent process results in omitting many of the psalms. It also can slow your devotional momentum as you find yourself aimlessly meandering through chapters instead of praying.

With the Psalms of the Day you take thirty seconds or so to quickly scan five specific psalms and pick the one that best leads you to prayer on that occasion. It's based on taking the 150 psalms and dividing them by thirty days (because most months have at least thirty days). That results in five psalms per day. (If bringing math into prayer is making you skeptical, stay with me! There's a simple chart in the back of the book that may visually convey all you'll need to understand what I'm trying to describe.)

Or to put it another way, if you were to read five psalms a day for an entire month, at the end of the month you would have read through the entire book of Psalms. While reading five psalms a day is a great practice that many enjoy, that's not what I'm advocating here. What I'm suggesting is that you take half a minute to quickly *scan* five psalms and pick one of those five to pray through.

Here's how it works. The first psalm is the one that corresponds with the day of the month. If today is the fifteenth of the month, then your first psalm would be Psalm 15. On the fifteenth day of the month you start with the fifteenth psalm.

To get your second psalm, you simply add thirty. Why thirty? Because there are thirty days in the month. So thirty added to fifteen is forty-five. Thus the second psalm you would scan on the fifteenth of the month would be Psalm 45.

After that you just keep adding thirty until you get your

five psalms. So thirty added to Psalm 45 takes you to Psalm 75, and thirty more to Psalm 105, and then thirty more to Psalm 135. So on the fifteenth of the month the Psalms of the Day are 15; 45; 75; 105; and 135. Those five psalms are the Psalms of the Day on the fifteenth of every month. So on the fifteenth day of this month, next month, and the month after that, you take thirty seconds to scan Psalms 15; 45; 75; 105; and 135, and then pick one of those five as the psalm you pray through.

What psalm do you use on the thirty-first of a month? That's when you pray through part (or all if you have time!) of Psalm 119. Of course, Psalm 119 will come up on the twenty-ninth, for the Psalms of the Day on the twenty-ninth are 29; 59; 89; 119; and 149. But even if you decide to use Psalm 119 on the twenty-ninth, because of its length chances are that there will be unused portions of the psalm that you can pray through on the thirty-first.

Since I'm a professor, I'm going to give you a pop quiz here. What are the Psalms of the Day for *today*?

Did you get them? Again, if you need to, refer to the chart in the back of the book to confirm that you understand how to identify the five Psalms of the Day on any day of the month.

The Benefits

As we've learned, the most important benefit of this little plan is that it gives you direction and momentum. No matter how tired, sleepy, or distracted you might be when you go to pray, with this method you know on any given day exactly which five psalms you will consider. And it helps you avoid saying, "Let's see. What psalm should I use today? Hmmmm, how about this one? No, I read that one the other day. Then maybe this one? No, I don't really like that one." Instead of helping the heart soar in prayer, such an unordered approach tends to pour sludge into the soul. Usually it's far better to know immediately which psalms you will scan.

A second benefit of using the Psalms of the Day plan is that by it you regularly and systematically encounter each of the 150 psalms. All the psalms are equally inspired, and all are worthy of your consideration in prayer. They are not all equally easy to pray through—the imprecatory psalms are more challenging to use in prayer than Psalm 23—but they are equally God-breathed. And if you will take thirty seconds to review five psalms every day, it is uncanny how one of them will express something that is looking for expression in your heart.

Praying a "Psalm of the Day"

Having explained how to find the Psalms of the Day, now let's use it to review the main point of the book, which is to actually pray through Scripture, in this case, one of those five psalms. Suppose today is the twentieth of the month. The Psalms of the Day are 20; 50; 80; 110; and 140. After a quick scan of them, let's say you settle on Psalm 20 as the one you want to pray through. So you might read the beginning of verse 1—"May the LORD answer you in the day of trouble!"—and pray:

> Lord, please answer me today. I am in trouble—my finances are in trouble, my body is in trouble, and my relationships are in trouble. O answer me today, Lord, because I am in trouble in so many ways.

Then you read the second half of verse 1: "May the name of the God of Jacob protect you!" That prompts you to pray something like this:

> Thank you, God of Jacob, that through your Son, Jesus, you have set me securely on high by your grace. I will never fall. By your work of preserving me through the Holy Spirit, I am securely set on high. The Bible says in Ephesians that I am seated in the heavenly places with Christ. Thank you for the security of that and all you have done for me in Christ.

As you pray these things, perhaps you already begin to sense your faith strengthening. Your confidence that the Lord will indeed answer grows as you ask him to answer you, not because of the earnestness of your pleading but because of the reality that he has set you securely on high in Christ. Indeed, as Australian theologian Graeme Goldsworthy put it, "As you pray a psalm, think about the pathway from the psalm to you through the mediation of Christ."[6]

Eagerly you turn to verse 2 and read, "May he send you help from the sanctuary." You pray:

> O God, send me help today right from the sanctuary of heaven itself. Send me help with my finances, send me help with my children, send me help in my work. From the highest place of authority that exists, send me help with my lack of faith. Send me heavenly help with temptation today. Please send me help right from the throne room of heaven, O Lord.

You might pray for heavenly help for many things, and then you read verse 3: "May he remember all your offerings and regard with favor your burnt sacrifices!" This might suggest to you words such as these:

> Heavenly Father, my offerings to you are the life and death of Jesus, your perfect Son. He is the offering you accept. Jesus is the sacrifice you will receive. I do give myself to you afresh, Lord—all that I am and all that I have. But I know that you will regard these with favor, and I believe you will hear my prayer for help from the sanctuary, because I offer them all in the name of the perfect offering, Jesus.

And thus you continue through the psalm until you run out of time or you run out of psalm.

The Psalms—Like a Little Bible

Book for book, I believe the best place in the Bible to pray the Bible is the book of Psalms. One reason for this, as someone has said, is that "the Psalms are like a little Bible. Every doctrine in the Bible is there: either in the bud or in the flower, but they are all there."

Another reason the Psalms adapt so easily to prayer is that God has inspired a psalm for every sigh of the soul. Within the breadth of 150 psalms, you can find the entire range of human emotion. You will never go through anything in life in which you cannot find the root emotions reflected in the Psalms. Exhilaration, frustration, discouragement, guilt, forgiveness, joy, gratitude, dealing with enemies, contentment, discontentment—you name it: they are all found in the book of Psalms. Athanasius, a fourth-century, North African theologian who famously defended the doctrine of the Trinity, said of the Psalms, "Whatever your particular need or trouble, from this same book you can select a form of words to fit it."[7] That's why, if you will look briefly at just five psalms, at least one of them almost always puts into words the burden of your heart at the time.

But the main reason why the psalms work so well in prayer is that the very purpose God put them in his Word to us is for us to put them in our words to him.

It is possible, of course, to talk to God from any part of his Word. So let's turn our attention to how we can pray from other parts of the Bible besides the Psalms.

6

Praying Other Parts
of the Bible

*For me it is absolutely essential that my prayers be
guided by, saturated by, and sustained and controlled
by the word of God.*

John Piper

In my experience, only the Psalms surpass the New Testament letters for the ease in which they can be turned into prayer. For starters, many of the New Testament letters contain prayers of the apostle Paul, which believers today can pray exactly as they are printed in the text (e.g., Eph. 1:15–23; 3:14–21; Phil. 1:9–11). Also, most of the content of these letters is such that little effort is needed to personalize them in prayer. So while many of the psalms address the Lord directly and can be prayed verbatim (such as Psalm 18:1, "I love you, O Lord, my strength"), the

New Testament letters usually require only a little more transition. For example, although Romans 8:1, "There is therefore now no condemnation for those who are in Christ Jesus," does not directly address the Lord, turning that verse into prayer requires nothing more than words such as, "Thank you, Lord, that I am free from condemnation because of Christ Jesus."

New Testament Letter

Let's look at how praying through several verses together in a New Testament letter might go. Suppose the passage you choose is 1 Thessalonians 2.[8] But why, it might be asked, would someone want to pray through 1 Thessalonians 2, especially if the Psalms are so well suited for prayer?

One reason is that someone might decide to pray through 1 Thessalonians 2 precisely because they know what it says and believe that the subject matter of that chapter is what they need to pray about, just as the person who feels the need for a more loving heart and would know to turn to 1 Corinthians 13 in order to pray about that.

Far more likely, though, is that a person might decide to pray through 1 Thessalonians 2 simply because his daily Bible reading has taken him to that chapter. After reading the chapter he decides, "This really ministered to me, so instead of going to the Psalms to pray, I'll stay in this chapter and pray through what I just read."

Having settled on 1 Thessalonians 2, you read verse 1: "For you yourselves know, brothers, that our coming to you was not in vain." Then perhaps you pray:

Thank you, Lord, for the one who came to me with your gospel. Thank you for his/her faithfulness to share the words of eternal life in Jesus. Thank you for opening my eyes to my need for your salvation so that I did not receive your gospel in vain.

After you say all that comes to mind from verse 1, you turn to verse 2: "But though we had already suffered and been shamefully treated at Philippi, as you know . . ." The words "suffered and been shamefully treated" stand out to you because of the suffering in your own life at present. So you pray about matters related to your suffering and the relief of it. That may lead you to think of people in your family, church, or neighborhood who are suffering, so you pray for them. The words "shamefully treated" may also apply to you personally and prompt prayers about that. Further, they may bring to mind fellow believers near and far who are experiencing persecution for being followers of Jesus, individuals or people groups you've recently heard about at church or in the news.

Following those prayers, you continue reading in verse 2: ". . . We had boldness in our God to declare to you the gospel of God in the midst of much conflict." Afterward you may find yourself praying along these lines:

O God, give me the boldness to declare the gospel to that person at work, to that person down the street, despite the conflict in their heart. I pray for the Christians in the Sudan, in India, in China, in the places of persecution I just mentioned. Give them the boldness to declare the gospel despite the conflict they experience due to the government and false religions.

Once you've said all that comes to mind from verse 2, you look to the next verse: "For our appeal does not spring from error or impurity or any attempt to deceive." Almost immediately you might think of someone you know whose mind and heart are being clouded by error, a friend or family member who has become enamored with some false teacher. Or perhaps you pray for someone being tempted with impurity—you, your spouse, or your child. Then you pray for anyone you know who is falling prey to deception, possibly a young woman being deceived by a young man, or vice versa.

As you consider verse 3 again, you realize that Paul was saying that his teaching, in contrast to that of some others, did not spring from error or deception. So you pray for the teachers in your church, namely, that no error would infect their study and preparation and thereby infect the church. You pray that God would protect them from impurity and the damage that could do to the church. And you ask the Lord to keep them free from all deception.

If you were to pray through 1 Thessalonians 2 in that way, how long would it take you to pray through those twenty verses? Quite awhile, right? Yet you wouldn't run out of anything to say, would you?

Have you ever had the problem of running out of things to say in prayer? D. A. Carson, in his excellent book on the prayers of the apostle Paul, presents a solution:

> Pray over the Scriptures. Christians just setting out on the path of prayer sometimes pray for everything they can think of, glance at their watches, and discover they have been at it for all of three or four minutes. This experience sometimes generates feelings of defeat, discouragement, even despair. A great way to begin to overcome this problem is to pray through various biblical passages.[9]

But best of all, if you were to pray through 1 Thessalonians 2 verse by verse, as illustrated above, not only would you have no shortage of things to say but also your prayer would be unlike any you have ever prayed in your life. Make it your prayer practice to pray the Bible, and you'll never again say the same old things about the same old things.

The New Testament letters constitute such a rich resource for prayer because you find so much packed into almost every verse. In 1 Thessalonians 2:2, for example, even between the commas we discover matter for prayer. Virtually every line in a New Testament letter suggests something to pray about. In fact, as we've already noted, many of these letters include actual prayers. But now we've learned that we can pray not only through the prayers but through every part of the letters, from the opening greeting to the final blessing.

Narrative

Let's look now at how to pray through one other genre of literature in the Bible, a narrative passage. To do that, let's turn to John 5.

We certainly need to learn to pray through narrative passages because so much of the Bible is narrative—especially in the Gospels, the book of Acts, and all those Old Testament stories. But there is one big difference between praying through a narrative passage and praying through a psalm or a New Testament letter. Thus far we have looked at the text microscopically. In Psalm 23 we read, "The LORD is my shepherd," and we took note earlier of someone who read those five words and prayed about them for twenty-five minutes. In 1 Thessalonians 2:2 we prayed about several items prompted just by words found between two commas in the same sentence. But in a narrative passage, instead of leaning over the text and looking at it microscopically, we need to back up and get the big picture.

Just think about what would be involved in praying microscopically over a narrative passage such as John 5, which begins: "After this there was a feast of the Jews" (v. 1). Well, if you had to pray about something there, you might eventually think of some way to pray about feasting, or confess that you've feasted too much lately—but it

wouldn't be easy, would it? Instead, what you would probably do is read all eight verses in this story and pray about
the big ideas, that is, the big, broad brushstrokes of the
narrative. That's because in a narrative passage of Scripture
there are typically stage-setting verses, after which comes
the punch line of the story. It may be only the punch line
that you pray about in a narrative passage.

So in the case of John 5, the mention of "a multitude
of invalids—blind, lame, and paralyzed" (v. 4) would likely
lead you to pray for someone you know who needs healing.
Perhaps verse 5, "One man was there who had been an in-
valid for thirty-eight years," would cause you to remember
and pray for a friend or family member who has suffered
with an illness or a disability for a very long time. Maybe
then you reflect on how easy it is to become accustomed
to the suffering of others as opposed to the mercy of Jesus,
shown here in healing this man, and you pray for forgiveness and a more Christlike attitude. Most of all, this brief
paragraph may cause you to realize afresh how gentle Jesus
is to sinners who feel hopeless and powerless about their
condition but who look to him for mercy. This might prompt
you not only to look anew to Jesus for mercy and forgiveness
for yourself but also to pray that others you know—perhaps
that one who needs healing—would look to Jesus for mercy.

Once you have prayed through a section of Scripture,
I'm confident you can turn to any part of the Bible and pray
through that passage.

7

The Most Important Part of This Book

The Psalms are given us to this end, that we may learn to pray them in the name of Jesus Christ.

Dietrich Bonhoeffer

Having walked the path of this book thus far, now you find yourself at a fork in this trail of words. In one direction the path is called "Information"; the other is called "Transformation." At this juncture you will decide whether the pages you've turned (and those ahead) will change your life or be forgotten, whether a transformation in prayer occurs or you add this book to the pile of those you've read but do not remember.

That's because I'm going to ask you now to put down this book, pick up your Bible, and pray through a psalm. Choose one of the Psalms of the Day or just pick a favorite.

Well-known psalms such as 23; 27; 31; 37; 42; 66; 103; or 139 also make good choices for this exercise.

Have you chosen your psalm? Good! If not, go back and reread the two preceding paragraphs.

Do you have one now? No? Then please stop reading and choose a psalm. Perhaps you are thinking, "Nah, I'll just keep reading and pray later." Having taught this material hundreds of times, I know by repeated experience that those who fail to do this exercise soon forget the teaching and profit little from having encountered it.

You are reading this book because you want a richer, more satisfying experience with God in prayer, right? But this book won't help you unless you apply its teaching to your prayer life. And that's what I'm asking you to do right now—not someday, but now—to apply what you've learned by praying through a psalm. So if you haven't already done so, select a psalm now.

Ready? If so, I'd like you to try praying through the psalm for at least seven minutes. It doesn't matter whether you sit, kneel, or walk as you pray.[10] Check the time—use a timer if possible so you won't be distracted by looking at the time—and begin.

8

Evaluating the Experience

For freshness of utterance, for breadth of comprehension, for elevation of thought, for intimacy of heart, there is no prayer like that which forms itself in the words and thoughts of Scripture.

J. Graham Miller

Okay, welcome back. Wait—you *did* pray through a psalm, didn't you? Good! You'll be able to identify with this section only if you engaged in the exercise.

So, how did it go? Unfortunately, I can't converse with you in person about your experience, but if I could, I have a pretty good idea of the kinds of things you would say. That's because whenever I've asked, "How did it go?" to a group who has just prayed through a psalm, I always get the same kinds of responses. Below are some of the most common.

"My Mind Didn't Wander"

It's much easier to remain focused in prayer when you pray your way through a passage. With the text to hold your attention and guide you in prayer, your thoughts are less likely to dissolve into the almost mindless repetition of the same old things about the same old things. And when you've finished praying about a certain matter, or even if your mind does begin to wander, the next verse in the text makes it easy for you to refocus.

"My Prayer Was More about God and Less about Me"

Praying through a passage of Scripture—especially a psalm—tends to be a more God-centered way of praying. People report that they find themselves praising God more than usual. Instead of prayer being mostly a time of saying, in effect, "Lord, here I am again with my usual list of the things I want you to do for me," it becomes more about God—his attributes, his ways, and his will. And more God-centered prayer is a good thing, isn't it?

In an effort to make prayer less self-centered and to give some sense of order to their prayers, many have adopted the well-known ACTS acrostic. Using this memory aid, you begin your prayer with "A" (adoration), then continue with "C" (confession), followed by "T" (thanksgiving), and only then "S" (supplication). While the structure can be helpful, the problem is that after awhile this method also produces the same repetitious prayers.

So although we want to be God-centered in prayer and begin with "A" (adoration), the tendency is to ask ourselves, "How should I adore the Lord today?" And since we don't have the time or the mental resources to think every day of new ways to adore the Lord, we tend to fall back on the same old ways, words, and phrases we habitually use to adore the Lord.

The good news is that you don't have to come up with new ways to adore the Lord. The Lord has given us 150 chapters of divinely inspired praises (that is, the Psalms) for us to use in adoration. Praying these will bend our prayers more toward God and less toward ourselves. Moreover, praying the Psalms will lead us to confession, thanksgiving, and supplication as well.[11]

"The Time Was Too Short!"

I get excited when I hear this comment, and so do the pastors who hear their people say such things after the exercise. "That was seven minutes?" people will ask. "It felt like two or three!" Some will admit, "I'm ashamed to say it, but I can't remember the last time I prayed for seven full minutes. And yet I could have kept going a lot longer."

If this was your experience, you also know that even if you had continued in prayer, you would not have run out of things to say. All that's needed is simply to carry on to the next verse, then the next verse, and so on, as long as you have time.

"Some people wonder how you can pray longer than five minutes," says John Piper, "because they would lose things to pray for. But I say that if you open the Bible, start reading it, and pause at every verse and turn it into a prayer, then you can pray all day that way."[12]

"It Seemed Like a Real Conversation with a Real Person"

That's what prayer is, remember? Prayer *is* talking with a person, the person of God himself. So prayer shouldn't be considered a one-way conversation. And yet, somehow, many people assume that when they meet with God, they must do all the talking.

"Lord, please hear me, for I've come again to talk about what *I* want to talk about and to ask you to give to me and do for me the same things as always."

Of course, we'd never speak so crassly to God, but in effect that's exactly what we do. Since we typically want to pray about the same things almost every day, and because we usually don't have the time or creative energy to think either of new directions to go in prayer or of different ways to talk with God about our daily concerns, we end up saying the same old things about the same old things. Perhaps we imagine the Lord folding his arms, silently enduring the next installment of our repetitious monologue.

When we pray the Bible, though, our monologue *to* God becomes a conversation *with* God. I'm not alluding to the perception of some spiritual impression or hearing an inner voice, imagining God saying things to us—away with that sort of mysticism. Instead, I'm referring to the Bible as the means by which God enters the conversation, for the Bible *is* God speaking.

So when you read verse 1 of a psalm, even though the words were originally put on paper by a man, the inspiration of Scripture—that is, God the Holy Spirit inspiring the man to write exactly what he (God) wanted—means that ultimately God is speaking in verse 1. And then you respond by speaking to God about what he's just said in verse 1. After you've finished talking, you do as you do in a real conversation with a real person: you let the other person speak again. In this case, letting the other person speak is called "reading verse 2." If something God says there prompts a reply, then you speak to him again.

That's why people who try this often report, "The pressure was off. I didn't have to think about what to say next, and it just kind of flowed."

Unlike the difficulties of trying to talk with a poor conversationalist, you don't have to initiate this conversation or feel the awkward responsibility of keeping it going when you can't think of anything to say. God begins the dialogue by speaking to you in verse 1. You simply respond to what he initiates. When you've finished, God bears the burden of continuing the conversation from there, for he speaks again in the next verse, and the cycle begins again. And God is willing to continue this conversation with you as long as you want and to have another with you whenever you want.

"The Psalm Spoke Directly to the Life Situation I Am in Right Now"

If you will quickly scan five psalms, it is indeed amazing how often at least one of them applies to the major concern of your life at the moment. The psalms were written by men of flesh and blood who were also men of God. They experienced real struggles and hard trials, just as we do. You don't have to read very far before you find their words becoming your words and their hearts expressing your heart.

"I Thought More Deeply about What the Bible Says"

One of the many reasons I love praying the Bible is that not only is it a method of prayer; it is also a method of meditation on Scripture. You read the verse, think about it for a moment, talk to God about it, then perhaps you look at it again and go through the process once more. By so doing, you are not only praying the Bible; you are absorbing it.

The conference I lead most frequently in local churches and retreats typically focuses Friday night on praying the

Bible, and Saturday morning on Scripture meditation. Late Saturday morning, when I'm teaching various ways to meditate on a text of Scripture,[13] I suggest praying the Bible as one of those ways. When I come to this point, I remind the participants about the brief exercise from the night before, when they spent just seven minutes or so praying through a psalm. Then I'll ask how many can recall at least a phrase from that psalm. It never fails that the vast majority can remember a line from a psalm they prayed through some fourteen hours earlier. What's really amazing is that these people also say that normally they can't remember anything they read in the Bible, even immediately upon closing the cover. But now they testify that they have actually memorized all or part of a verse they read the night before.

And they've slept since then.

And they spent no more than seven minutes on the passage (and probably only a few of those seven minutes were spent on the verse they remember).

And they were tired when they prayed through the psalm (which was done about 8:30 p.m. on Friday, often the most weary night of the week).

And they weren't trying to memorize anything—but they did.

And they didn't know they were going to have a pop quiz the next morning.

I've actually seen people weep at this point and say, "I can remember the Bible!"

When you remember what you encounter in the Bible, you are far more likely to think deeply about what it says, not only while you are praying but also at random moments all through your day, and thus to "meditate on it day and night," as described in Joshua 1:8 and Psalm 1:2.

How about you? Can you remember a phrase from the psalm you prayed through during the exercise a few minutes ago? If you can remember a line you read in the psalm fifteen minutes ago, you'll probably be able to remember it on your way to work, while waiting in line during the noon hour, and if you wake up in the middle of the night. During unscheduled occasions, "day and night" you'll find yourself able to say, "Now, what was that verse? Oh, yeah, I remember." And you'll be able to think about it some more or pray about it again.

So simple. Such sustained profit from a very short time in the Scripture. And with very little effort.

You can do this. In fact, I no longer have to persuade you that you *can* do this, for if you did the exercise, I'm confident you have already testified to me (in response to my question above, "Can you remember a phrase from the psalm you prayed through during the exercise?") that you *have* done it, that is, you *have* remembered something you read in the Bible several minutes ago and did so without a special effort to memorize it. Be encouraged, my brother or sister! This should convince you that if you have the Bible and the Holy Spirit, you have all the equipment necessary to profit satisfyingly from the Word of God and to experience a meaningful prayer life.

"I Had Greater Assurance That I Was Praying God's Will"

The Bible makes plain in 1 John 5:14–15 that we must pray according to the will of God if we expect him to answer:

> This is the confidence that we have toward him, that if we ask anything according to his will he hears us. And if we know that he hears us in whatever we ask, we know that we have the requests that we have asked of him.

Since it is so important to pray in conformity with God's will, can you have any greater assurance that you are praying the will of God than when you are praying the Word of God?

That doesn't mean that praying the Bible ensures that we'll never misinterpret or misapply the Bible as we pray, thinking we are praying the will of God when we are not. Nevertheless, what better way to discern God's will and to conform our prayers to God's will than to pray God's Word?

"I Prayed about Things I Normally Don't Pray About"

This is one of the most common responses I hear. When you pray through a passage of Scripture, you'll often find yourself praying about matters that would never come to mind otherwise. You will intercede for people and situations you would not think to include on a prayer list even if you made one as long as the New York City phone directory.[14] You'll pray for national or international events, world leaders, unreached people groups, people you live near or work with, ministers and missionaries, long-forgotten places, and people you've not encountered in years.

Another time, when I was teaching this in California, a woman I'll call Jenny told me on Saturday morning what had happened to her during and after the exercise on Friday night. Something in the psalm through which she was praying brought to mind a friend—I'll call her Pam—she had known in New York prior to moving to California fifteen years earlier. Jenny had not heard once in any way from Pam in a decade and a half. Nevertheless, when Pam came to mind during the exercise, Jenny prayed for her. After Jenny got home that evening, Pam called her from across the country, reaching out for the first time in fifteen years, anxious to talk about spiritual matters.

God's mind and God's Word are so much broader than our own perspective, and he will prompt you through the Bible to pray with an awareness for things far beyond the same old things.

"I Prayed about the Things I Normally Do Pray about but in New and Different Ways"

This is also one of the most frequent replies I receive when I ask, "How did it go?" When you pray the Bible, you'll still bring to the Lord the same matters you always pray about—your family, the future, finances, work, school, church, ministry, Christian concerns, and the current crisis—but you'll pray about them in fresh ways almost every time.

At the seminary I begin every class with Scripture reading and prayer. I make essentially the same request every time: "Lord, please bless this class." How many different ways can you think of to pray, "Lord, please bless this class"? But I use this occasion to model praying the Bible for my students. So I'll read one of the Psalms of the Day and begin praying through part of it. If I ask God through Psalm 23 to bless the class, then my prayer becomes, "Lord, please shepherd us in this class today." That same request prayed through Psalm 51 is, "Lord, please forgive us for not always applying our minds to our studies as we ought, but help us to do that today." If the psalm is 139, then the prayer is more like, "Lord, we acknowledge your presence here in room 102 today; you are the teacher here, and we ask you to teach us in this class." It's basically the same prayer ("please bless the class") on each occasion, and yet, because that prayer is prayed through a different psalm every day, it's a different prayer in every class.

I believe it's good for me to ask the Lord's blessing in every class, just as I believe there are a number of matters in other parts of my life about which it is good to pray every day. You surely have your own set of good and regular requests. The way to transform them from a routine recitation into a mindful, heartfelt petition is to send them heavenward through a different passage of Scripture each time.

"I Didn't Say the Same Old Things about the Same Old Things"

This is best of all. It bears repeating that a stale prayer life can experience a new freshness with a simple change of method. Anyone with a Bible and the Holy Spirit has everything necessary to enjoy God in prayer and to banish the boredom born of repeating tired phrases about the same old things.

Suppose you won a contest in which the grand prize was the opportunity to spend an hour in conversation with any person of your choosing. For a full hour, you could ask any question and talk about whatever you wanted with any person in the world. Whom would you choose? The president of the United States? A world leader? A famous singer, musician, or actor? An influential Christian? One of the world's best-known athletes? A preeminent scientist or scholar? A best-selling author? A possible romantic interest?

What if I said, "Great news! A one-hour conversation between you and that person has been arranged for tomorrow morning." Tonight you'd hardly be able to sleep because of the anticipation. Then suppose that the conversation proved to be everything you imagined, and afterward I said, "Great news! Tomorrow you get to have another hour-long conversation with that person. The only caveat is that both of you must say exactly the same things you said today."

Hmmm. Well, you might pick up a few things in that second conversation that didn't register with you the first time. But what if you had to have that same conversation every day for the rest of your life? It probably wouldn't be long before you'd rather die than endure that conversation again.

It's a sad truth, but we can feel the same way even about talking with God. You can be talking to the most interesting Person in the universe about the most important things in your life and be bored to death. Is that because you don't love God? No. Is it because you don't love what you are praying about? No. It's because you have essentially the same conversation about those things every day. If you do that, even talking with God himself can be boring.

But now you have a solution. Let God initiate the conversation by means of your Bible, and you simply respond to his words there. Isn't that easy? Anyone can do that.

If You Teach This to Others

If you ever teach these things to a group of believers, be sure you do two things.

First and most importantly, give your listeners an opportunity to try praying through a passage of Scripture right then. In other words, don't teach them how to pray the Bible in one session and then wait to have them try it in the next day's or the next week's session, because after you teach them, they'll say, "That's a great idea. I'll have to try that someday." But they never will.

However, if you'll give them a few minutes to actually experience praying the Bible, then, just like you, many of them will be hooked. Also, like you, they will never again pray the same old things about the same old things. They will not need any notes to remember how to do it. Like riding a bicycle, once they learn how, they'll never forget. It couldn't be simpler: just open up the Bible and talk to God.

Second, immediately after the prayer exercise, ask for some feedback. I've always found that as people report their experience, their excitement becomes contagious. And not only will the participants encourage one another through their testimonies, but also each of their comments will provide you with an occasion to respond with additional insights into the practice, just as I've illustrated above.

So give people an opportunity to experience praying through Scripture, then ask them to talk about the experience.

9

What Have We Learned?

Praying the Word means reading (or reciting) Scrip-
ture in a spirit of prayer and letting the meaning of the
verses become our prayer and inspire our thoughts.

John Piper

So what have we learned? We've recognized the almost universal tendency to pray the same old things about the same old things and that such prayer is boring. When prayer is boring, we don't feel like praying. And when we don't feel like praying, we find it very hard to pray. When we have to compel ourselves to pray, our prayers are joyless, our minds wander, and a very few minutes in prayer seems like hours. As a result we feel like spiritual failures, certain that we are second-rate Christians.

But now we've learned that instead of saying the same old, gray, colorless prayers, we can pray in fresh, new ways about almost everything we pray about virtually every time we pray.

A woman, let's say, who wants to pray every day for her children or grandchildren might pray for them today as she prays through Psalm 23. This text prompts her to pray that God "shepherd" her children in various ways, and there's something about that shepherding imagery that transforms the same old things she usually prays into a dynamic new prayer enriched with the inspired words of God.

Tomorrow she might pray through 1 Corinthians 13, and doing so leads her to ask the Lord to develop in her children the kind of love taught in that chapter. The next day, while making her way through Psalm 1, the text guides her to pray that her children would become meditators on the Word of God. Isn't that a wonderful thing to pray for your children? But would you ever pray that if you didn't pray through Psalm 1? The following day she finds herself in Galatians 5 and pleads with the Lord to develop the fruit of the Spirit in her children. After that she's back in the Psalms, and while conversing with the Lord through Psalm 139, she asks that her children would sense his presence wherever they go that day.

In reality, the heart of her prayer—"Bless my children"—remains unchanged, even though her words change. By filtering that prayer through a different passage of Scripture each time, her prayer changes from a mind-numbing repetition of the same old things to a request that ascends from her heart to heaven in unique ways every day.

10

The Examples of George Mueller, Jesus on the Cross, and Christians in the Book of Acts

For thirty centuries, God's people have found in the Psalms an answer to the disciples' plea, "Lord, teach us to pray."

Ken Langley

George Mueller (1805–1898) is widely considered one of the greatest men of prayer and faith since the days of the New Testament. He lived nearly the entire nineteenth century, two-thirds of it in Bristol, England. He led four far-reaching, influential ministries, but we know him best today for his orphanages. During a time in England when most

81

orphans lived in miserable workhouses or on the streets, like Charles Dickens's Oliver Twist, Mueller took them in, fed them, clothed them, and educated them. Through his orphanage in Bristol, Mueller cared for as many as two thousand orphans at a time—more than ten thousand in his lifetime. Yet he never made the needs of his ministries known to anyone except to God in prayer. Only through his annual reports did people learn after the fact what the needs had been during the previous year and how God had provided.[15]

Mueller had over fifty thousand specific recorded answers to prayers in his journals, thirty thousand of which he said were answered the same day or the same hour that he prayed them. Think of it: that's five hundred definite answers to prayer each year—more than one per day—every single day for sixty years! God funneled over half a billion dollars (in today's dollars) through his hands in answer to prayer.

Mueller's Example

How did George Mueller pray? He said that for the first ten years of what he called his "life of faith"—referring not to when he was unknown but to ten years of trust in God and remarkable answers to prayer—he often struggled to get into the spirit of prayer, in other words, to really feel like praying. Until, that is, he made one slight alteration in his method. Here's how he described the change:

The difference, then, between my former practice and my present one is this: formerly, when I rose, I began to pray as soon as possible, and generally spent all my time till breakfast in prayer, or almost all the time. At all events I almost invariably began with prayer. . . . But what was the result? I often spent a quarter of an hour, or half an hour, or even an hour on my knees before being conscious to myself of having derived comfort, encouragement, humbling of soul, etc.; and often, after having suffered much from wandering of mind for the first ten minutes, or quarter of an hour, or even half an hour, I only then really began to pray.

I scarcely ever suffer now in this way. For my heart being nourished by the truth, being brought into experimental [today we would say "experiential"] fellowship with God, I speak to my Father and to my Friend (vile though I am, and unworthy of it) about the things that He has brought before me in His precious Word. It often now astonishes me that I did not sooner see this point.[16]

So Mueller would sometimes flounder for half an hour to an hour trying to pray, fighting to focus his thoughts and to kindle feelings for prayer in his heart. Only after that long, determined struggle would he finally enter into a sense of communion with God. But once he began the practice of conversing with God about what he found in the Word of God, he "scarcely ever" suffered with those problems in prayer again.

Praying through a passage of Scripture as he went "walking about in the fields"[17] was the uncomplicated method that transformed the daily experience of one of the most famous men of prayer in history. And it can transform *your* prayer life just as easily.

Charles Spurgeon (1834–1892), the British Baptist often called "the prince of preachers," said in regard to feelings in prayer: "We should pray when we are in a praying mood, for it would be sinful to neglect so fair an opportunity. We should pray when we are not in a proper mood, for it would be dangerous to remain in so unhealthy a condition."[18] And he's right. We should pray when we feel like praying and pray when we don't feel like praying. But the reality, as I've argued throughout this book, is that most of the time when we go to prayer, we don't feel like praying.

If, say, you get up at 7:00 a.m. and go to pray, most days you probably don't feel like praying. Why? Because you're sleepy! You haven't been thinking about God and the things of God for the last several hours; you've been dead to the world. If you're at all the way I am in the morning, you don't wake up with your heart instantly on fire for God and the things of God. Personally, I tend to run into door frames when I get up. If even George Mueller didn't feel like praying when he got out of bed, don't be surprised if you don't.

The good news is that we are not subject to those feelings. God said to Jeremiah, "Is not my word like fire, declares the LORD?" (Jer. 23:29). If you go to pray and your heart is cold as ice spiritually, you can take the fire of God's Word and plunge it into your frosty heart by praying through a passage of Scripture. Then very soon, just as during that prayer exercise a short while ago, the Word of God warms your heart to the things of God, and you begin to feel like praying.

And I can testify to the fact that having prayed this way almost every day for more than thirty years,[19] there is nothing in my devotional life that more quickly and consistently kindles my consistently cold heart like praying the Bible.

Jesus on the Cross

But far more important than the testimony of George Mueller or anyone else is the example of Jesus himself praying the Psalms. On the cross Jesus said only seven brief things. The Roman soldiers had beaten him until ribbons of skin were flayed from his bloody back. He had barely been able to stagger to the place of crucifixion. He hung from the cross severely dehydrated. And with his entire body weight sagging on the three spikes that held him to the wood, he had to push up on the spike in his feet in order to get enough breath into his diaphragm so he could speak. But to do so was so agonizing that he could speak only briefly before sinking back down. If the Romans wanted to hasten the death of those they crucified, they would break the prisoners' legs so they couldn't push up and would die of asphyxiation. In fact, this is what they did to the two thieves at Jesus's side (see John 19:31–33).

Understandably, then, everything Jesus spoke from the cross was very brief. But the longest thing he said was, "My God, my God, why have you forsaken me?" (Matt. 27:46), which is the first verse of Psalm 22, the longest and most explicit prophecy in the Old Testament about the crucifixion. Psalm 22 contains more details about the physical aspects of crucifixion than all four Gospels combined.[20]

For example, in Psalm 22:14a the psalmist says, "I am poured out like water," just as the apostle John reported of Jesus in John 19:34–35. In 14b we read, "all my bones are out of joint," describing how the victims, after their limbs were twisted somewhat in order to nail them to the beams, often had their bones jarred out of joint as their heavy cross was dropped into the ground. And the words of verse 15b, "my tongue sticks to my jaws," were fulfilled in the cry of Jesus, "I thirst" (John 19:28).

In addition, what we read in Psalm 22:7—"All who see me mock me; they make mouths at me; they wag their heads"—is fulfilled in Matthew 27:39 when "those who passed by derided him, wagging their heads." Verse 8 introduces the voice of scoffers who say, "He trusts in the Lord; let him deliver him," which is the same scorn Jesus received in Matthew 27:43 from those who said, "He trusts in God; let God deliver him now." In Psalm 22:16 David describes the opposition of his enemies by saying, "For dogs encompass me; a company of evildoers encircles me," which accurately portrays those who were snipping and sniping at the Son of David around the foot of his cross.

Further, Psalm 22:17 quotes the psalmist as saying, "I can count all my bones," which would have been true of Jesus, since the Romans crucified people unclothed. The next verse says, "They divide my garments among them, and for my clothing they cast lots," which is exactly what the Roman soldiers did with the clothes of Jesus in Matthew 27:35.

So after Jesus heaves himself upward on the spike in his feet and cries out Godward with the first verse of Psalm 22, I am convinced that as he sank back down, he continued to pray through Psalm 22.[21] To some degree that is speculation, but we know that he prayed the first verse. We also know why he vocalized so little as he hung there. And since he was literally fulfilling Psalm 22 at that very moment, I believe it's more than reasonable to assume that after he prayed verse 1 aloud, Jesus sagged on the cross and silently continued to pray the rest of Psalm 22.

Then at the end, Jesus gathered the last ounce of his strength, strained upward a final time, and cried, "Father, into your hands I commit my spirit" (Luke 23:46), praying the words of Psalm 31:5.

Jesus prayed the Psalms. The final act of his earthly life was to pray the words of a psalm.

Christians in the Book of Acts

Then, in Acts 4, after Peter and John have been arrested and threatened by the Jewish authorities for preaching Christ, verse 23 says:

> When they were released, they went to their friends [that is, the church] and reported what the chief priests and the elders had said to them. And when they heard it, they lifted their voices together to God and said, "Sovereign Lord, who made the heaven and the earth and the sea and everything in them . . ."

In some translations the last half of verse 24 is punctuated to indicate that it is a quotation, for many scholars believe that these words were taken from Psalm 146:6.

In any case, notice how verse 25 continues: ". . . who through the mouth of our father David, your servant, said by the Holy Spirit, 'Why did the Gentiles rage, and the peoples plot in vain?'" The second half of that verse and all of the next are from Psalm 2 (vv. 1–2). In other words, the early church prayed the Psalms. And this is the place where we are told, "When they had prayed, the place in which they were gathered together was shaken, and they were all filled with the Holy Spirit and continued to speak the word of God with boldness" (v. 31).

These new Christians in Jerusalem, who had become believers on or soon after the day of Pentecost, prayed the Psalms. George Mueller, one of the most prayerful and faith-filled men in Christian history, prayed the Psalms. The Lord Jesus Christ himself prayed the Psalms. Why not you?

Appendix 1

"Psalms of the Day" Chart

When the day of the month is . . .	The Psalms of the Day are . . .
1	1; 31; 61; 91; 121
2	2; 32; 62; 92; 122
3	3; 33; 63; 93; 123
4	4; 34; 64; 94; 124
5	5; 35; 65; 95; 125
6	6; 36; 66; 96; 126
7	7; 37; 67; 97; 127
8	8; 38; 68; 98; 128
9	9; 39; 69; 99; 129
10	10; 40; 70; 100; 130
11	11; 41; 71; 101; 131
12	12; 42; 72; 102; 132
13	13; 43; 73; 103; 133
14	14; 44; 74; 104; 134
15	15; 45; 75; 105; 135
16	16; 46; 76; 106; 136
17	17; 47; 77; 107; 137
18	18; 48; 78; 108; 138

Appendix 1

When the day of the month is . . .	The Psalms of the Day are . . .
19	19; 49; 79; 109; 139
20	20; 50; 80; 110; 140
21	21; 51; 81; 111; 141
22	22; 52; 82; 112; 142
23	23; 53; 83; 113; 143
24	24; 54; 84; 114; 144
25	25; 55; 85; 115; 145
26	26; 56; 86; 116; 146
27	27; 57; 87; 117; 147
28	28; 58; 88; 118; 148
29	29; 59; 89; 119; 149
30	30; 60; 90; 120; 150
31	119

Appendix 2

Praying the Bible with a Group

Let the words and agenda of the Bible reverberate into your individual and corporate prayer life.

Jonathan Leeman

A group of Christians as well as individual believers can pray the Bible. The group can consist of a family, a class or Bible study, or even those at a church-wide prayer meeting. But whatever the purpose of the group or its size, don't try to lead a group to pray through a passage of Scripture until after the members have at least one experience in praying the Bible individually. Once they have an idea of what it's like to pray through a section of Scripture on their own, it's a lot easier for them to do so with others.

A Good Way

One good way to pray through a portion of the Bible with others is simply to assign a verse to every member of your group. The first person prays through the first verse, the second person prays as prompted by the second verse, the third person prays from the third verse, and so on. This works well until the verse that falls to someone in the group is one like, "Blessed shall he be who takes your little ones and dashes them against the rock!" (Ps. 137:9) or some other text that they do not understand or about which they can think of nothing to say. So this method can succeed, or it can backfire and embarrass people.

A Better Way

A better way is this: choose a psalm and read it aloud to your group or have everyone in your group read it silently. Ask each person to listen or look for one sentence or verse in particular that catches their attention. After the reading, ask all who will do so to pray audibly when they are ready and to begin their prayer by reading the line that attracted their attention. So every person starts by reading aloud the verse they have chosen; then they pray. That verse becomes the diving board into their prayer. This method works well as long as people pray close to their verse. If they drift from the verse, it often begins to sound like the same old things about the same old things.

The Best Way

Here's what I've found to be the best way: read the psalm and then call out, one at a time as needed, the verses or phrases from the psalm that you find most conducive to prayer. You simply pick verses easy to understand and which most anyone could pray from and pass over those verses that might be too difficult for some in your group.

So, for example, if you choose Psalm 37, you call out verses such as, "Trust in the LORD, and do good" (v. 3), and allow time for people to pick up on that and pray. When the group grows quiet, and it appears that no one else will pray, you read another verse aloud, perhaps skipping to one far down the page or in this case reading the next verse: "Delight yourself in the LORD, and he will give you the desires of your heart" (v. 4). Then, when it's needed, you introduce another verse or phrase from which almost anyone could pray, skipping over lines such as, "I have seen a wicked, ruthless man, spreading himself like a green laurel tree" (v. 35), because many would struggle with how to pray in response to those words.

Benefits

The primary benefit of praying this way with a group, just as with an individual, is that the prayers are fresh and more biblical. Apart from this method, if prayer requests are taken, and, say, prayer is asked for Josh, who lost his job, and for Jessica, who is scheduled for surgery, then the prayer for Josh is often routine, and the prayer for Jessica is basically the same one prayed last week for the person who was having surgery then. Moreover, regardless of the size of the group, only two people might pray, one for Josh and one for Jessica. This time, however, because you are praying through Psalm 37, someone prays that Josh would "trust in the Lord" as he looks for a job. Another prays that Josh would "do good" for the sake of the kingdom as he is waiting. Someone else prays that Jessica would "trust in the Lord" in the face of an uncertain outcome from the surgery. A fourth person prays that the church would "do good" in terms of ministering to both Josh and Jessica during this difficult time. When the next verse is given, people pray in various ways for both Josh and Jessica to receive the grace to delight themselves in the Lord in the midst of these challenging circumstances.

Not only do the prayers tend to be more scripturally sound, but also it seems that more people participate when a group prays through a passage of Scripture, as each successive verse sparks new things for people to pray. In addition, those who pray tend to use fewer filler words and also to pray more specifically for the request. Instead of the generic "Please bless this" and "Be with them" prayers, people pray things the Bible commands about particular people and situations.

Notes

1. Rom. 8:15, "For you did not receive the spirit of slavery to fall back into fear, but you have received the Spirit of adoption as sons, by whom we cry, 'Abba! Father!'"; Gal. 4:6, "And because you are sons, God has sent the Spirit of his Son into our hearts, crying, 'Abba! Father!'" And note that this heart cry is not merely something the Christian chooses to do but a new Godward look and longing caused by the Holy Spirit.
2. Although this verse has absolutely nothing to do with taking naps, shortly I will defend from Scripture the validity of *praying* virtually anything that comes to mind *while reading* the Scripture and distinguish this from *interpreting* Scripture, which must always be done rightly.
3. Andrew A. Bonar, *Memoir and Remains of Robert Murray M'Cheyne* (1844; repr. Edinburgh: Banner of Truth, 1978), 50, emphasis original.
4. Joni Eareckson Tada, *Speaking God's Language: Using the Word of God in Your Prayers* (Torrance, CA: Rose, 2012).
5. Although there is a wide variety of opinion on the correct interpretation of this triad (e.g., what, exactly, *is* a "spiritual song"), there is little disagreement that the phrase includes the inspired songs in Scripture, such as the book of Psalms.
6. Graeme Goldsworthy, *Prayer and the Knowledge of God: What the Whole Bible Teaches* (Downers Grove, IL: InterVarsity, 2004), 143.
7. Athanasius, *St. Athanasius on the Psalms: A Letter to a Friend*, (London: Mowbray, 1949), http://cs-people.bu.edu/butta1/personal/marcelli.htm (accessed November 2, 2014).
8. If we were to use Romans 8 or 1 Corinthians 13 or a similarly well-known chapter of the New Testament as our example, it might not be as instructive as looking at 1 Thessalonians 2 or another less familiar chapter. Most of the chapters in the New Testament

letters are probably not as well known to us as famous ones such as Romans 8 and 1 Corinthians 13. So to use an example such as 1 Thessalonians 2 is more like the kind of chapter you would ordinarily encounter if you wanted to pray through one of the letters you were reading in the New Testament.

9. D. A. Carson, *Praying with Paul: A Call to Spiritual Reformation*, 2nd ed. (Grand Rapids, MI: Baker Academic, 2014), 3.

10. Although you are likely engaging in this exercise in private, I've led groups as large as a thousand through it collectively. If you enjoy the opportunity to teach this material to others, it is possible for each individual to pray through a psalm even though surrounded by many others. Simply request that there be no whispering or any other unnecessary distractions. In some situations it may be possible for those who prefer to do so to move to another part of the room or to relocate to a vacant room or a place immediately outside the building. If you have the opportunity for a more extended time for the exercise, you might actually encourage people to go outside, weather permitting. When I teach this material in my seminary classes, I provide twenty to twenty-five minutes for this exercise, suggesting that all who want to may find a place to sit outdoors or walk slowly across campus as they pray.

11. Concern with including certain aspects of prayer, such as those found in the ACTS approach, raises the question of the "Model Prayer"—also known as "the Lord's Prayer"—found in Matt. 6:9–13 and Luke 11:1–14. How can we suggest that people utilize the Psalms or other parts of Scripture to guide our prayers when Jesus gave us an explicit model for prayer? In Luke 11:2 we do find justification for praying the words of the prayer verbatim, for Jesus says there, "When you pray, say: . . ." So it is a biblically sound practice, both in a private and a congregational context, to pray the Lord's Prayer. But in Matt. 6:9 Jesus says, "Pray then like this . . . " meaning that our prayers should be like or similar to that one. In other words, Jesus's prayer in Matt. 6:9–13 is an example or model of the way we should pray, a prayer that contains the elements of the kinds of prayer that pleases God. Clearly the apostles understood Jesus to be giving an example and not prescribing the only prayer his followers should pray, for we do not find them repeating these words in any of the prayers found elsewhere in the New Testament. For the purposes of this book, the point is that if a person regularly prays through passages of Scripture, he or she will be led by the text to pray the kinds of things Jesus includes in the Model

Prayer. Perhaps not each of the elements of the Model Prayer will be prompted by every text through which a person prays, but generally and routinely the Bible will bring before the praying Christian's mind everything found in the Model Prayer.

12. John Piper, "Should I Use the Bible When I Pray?," http://www.desiringgod.org/interviews/should-i-use-the-bible-when-i-pray (accessed October 31, 2014).

13. I describe seventeen different methods of meditation on Scripture in my *Spiritual Disciplines for the Christian Life* (Colorado Springs, CO: NavPress, 2014), 56–68.

14. How does one use a prayer list when praying the Bible? Some who pray the Bible do use a prayer list, while others simply let the text suggest their prayer list for that day. In other words, instead of organizing their prayer concerns by means of some sort of list, they pray with a more impromptu approach, speaking to God about whatever comes to mind as they read the text, unconcerned about whether they remember to pray about certain preplanned matters. If you are accustomed to praying with a list but, after experimenting with more spontaneity, you realize that you are not praying for certain people and situations as often as you'd like, then return to a prayer list. If you prefer a systematic plan, one way to incorporate that into praying through a passage of Scripture is to place your prayer list beside your Bible, and as you pray through the text, pray for those people on your list in accordance with what you read in the Bible. So, for example, if you pray through Psalm 23, when you read "The LORD is my shepherd," you ask, "Who on my prayer list needs shepherding?" Then when you read, "I shall not want," you pray for those on your list who are in want, and so on.

15. Of course, after reading these reports many were prompted to give to Mueller's ministries, so that the reports served indirectly as means through which Mueller raised support.

16. Roger Steer, ed., *Spiritual Secrets of George Muller* (Wheaton, IL: Harold Shaw, 1985), 62.

17. Ibid., 61.

18. C. H. Spurgeon, *The Salt Cellars: Being a Collection of Proverbs, Together with Homely Notes Thereon, Vol. I: A to L* (London: Passmore & Alabaster, 1889), 58.

19. From March 1, 1985, through the publication of this book in mid-2015.

20. While the Gospel writers describe a number of the things that occurred in connection with the crucifixion, such as the mockeries of

the Jewish leaders, the activities of the soldiers, or the words uttered by the two thieves crucified with Jesus, they actually provide very little explicit information about his physical sufferings, such as the kind revealed when he said, "I thirst" (John 19:28).

21. British Bible commentator Gordon Wenham goes further: "It has been suggested that our Lord was just praying his way through the Psalms as he hung on the cross. . . . This would have been a very appropriate thing to do, for so many of the early psalms are the prayers of a good man suffering and crying to God for help." Gordon Wenham, *The Psalter Reclaimed: Praying and Praising with the Psalms* (Wheaton, IL: Crossway, 2013), 38–39.

General Index

Scripture Index

About the Author

Don Whitney has been professor of biblical spirituality and associate dean at the Southern Baptist Theological Seminary in Louisville, Kentucky since 2005. He is also the founder and president of the Center for Biblical Spirituality.

Don graduated from Southwestern Baptist Theological Seminary in Fort Worth, Texas, with a Master of Divinity degree in 1979. In 1987, he completed a Doctor of Ministry degree at Trinity Evangelical Divinity School in Deerfield, Illinois and later a doctorate in theology at the University of the Free State in South Africa. Prior to his ministry as a seminary professor, Don was pastor of Glenfield Baptist Church in Glen Ellyn, Illinois (a suburb of Chicago), for almost fifteen years. Altogether, he has served local churches in pastoral ministry for twenty-four years.

Don is the author of *Spiritual Disciplines for the Christian Life* (NavPress, 1991), *How Can I Be Sure I'm a Christian?* (NavPress, 1994), *Spiritual Disciplines within the Church* (Moody Press, 1996), *Ten Questions to Diagnose Your Spiritual Health* (NavPress, 2001), and *Simplify Your Spiritual Life* (NavPress, 2003).

Don and his wife, Caffy, live near Louisville, Kentucky, and have one grown daughter, Laurelen Christiana.

Learn more about Don:

Website: BiblicalSpirituality.org
Twitter: twitter.com/DonWhitney
Facebook: facebook.com/DonWhitney